LOVE

smile

Poems by Wagner Anarca, "Papis"
Illustrations by "Mónica Ortiz García"

Copyright © 2016 by Wagner Anarca, "Papis". 735089

ISBN: Softcover   978-1-5144-5911-9
        EBook   978-1-5144-5910-2

All rights reserved. No part of this book may be reproduced or transmitted in any form or by any means, electronic or mechanical, including photocopying, recording, or by any information storage and retrieval system, without permission in writing from the copyright owner.

Print information available on the last page

Rev. date: 02/09/2016

To order additional copies of this book, contact:
Xlibris
1-888-795-4274
www.Xlibris.com
Orders@Xlibris.com

Introduction

"Love"

Own such a strong, deep and

Value meaning, which I could never

Ever express only by poems…

Meaning that I was looking for to share for

Other than myself…

Now I finally find.

Illustrations by a

Cheerful, Talent and Kind Artist from Badajoz, Spain…

Amazing Sensibility Art by "Mónica Ortiz García"

Thank you kindly my Dear…

Wagner Anarca "Papis"

Love shall

get there

someday…

Love
Has
A Mind of
Its
Own...

Love is a Butterfly's Cage...

I Love you even before I knew it...

It is in the air…

Dancing Souls
Flying Desires
Smiling Hearts
Thoughts on Fire

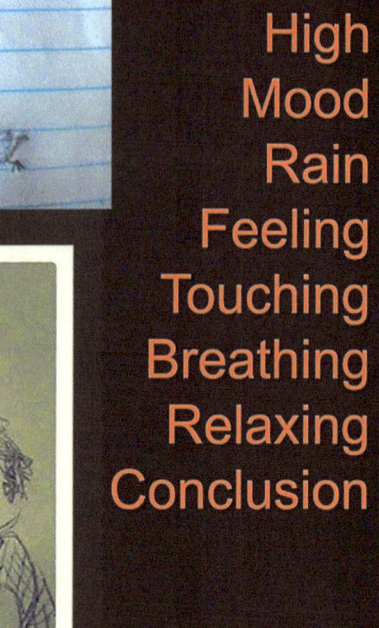

Love
World
Planet
Inside
Butterfly
Heart
High
Mood
Rain
Feeling
Touching
Breathing
Relaxing
Conclusion

Walking
Holding hands
Looking
Smiling
Smelling
Swimming
Felling
Sand
On my feet…

Love could get you a smile!!!

The Sky is Blue
My Desire is you!

Ardilla
Para nada!!
Lluvia
Bañarse
Sol
Trabajo
Otro
Copas
Viejo
Feo
Gordo
Regaños
Ehhh!!!
Grrr...
Pinocho
Nariz
Parado
Fantasias
Cariño

Love is a thing
That thinks
By itself

It is a form of energy
Beside us

It is all over
It is all over

Tomorrow
I Will
Remember
This...

I love you
Because the sun is shining and
The world is round

One who never loves
Never knows
What living is

So, keep on loving...

merienda con fresas.

Music
Lovers
Music
Lovers

*Smells like love,
Fells like you,
Listen to your Heart,
Touching your soul,
Whisper kisses...*

Ask me
Ask me
Ask me
But
You
Already
Know

*Do you know?
Sometimes when you are
Feeling Blue?
You want to do
Something...
Looking at sky
With no reason,
Smiling,
Yes!!!
You are in Love.*

*Never
Ever
Ever
Ever
But,
Only
You!*

Buenos días!!

*When you are in love,
The whole Universe
Is very Limited...
There is no time
For anything else*

Human being could live about 100 years.
Just to learn how to love...
That is why dogs would live only 15 year...

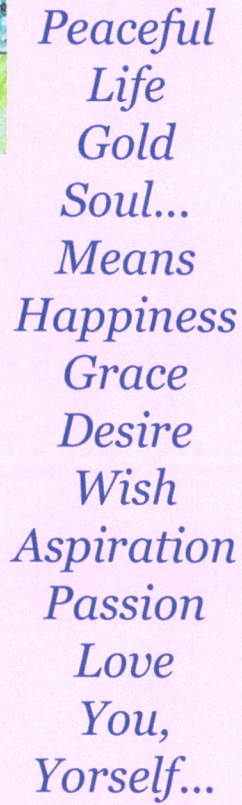

*Peaceful
Mind,
Peaceful
Life
Gold
Soul...
Means
Happiness
Grace
Desire
Wish
Aspiration
Passion
Love
You,
Yorself...*

25

*It's true...
You're asking me
About
The weather...
But don't live me in the rain...*

Sometimes
You love
Sometimes
You like
It is time to see
What loves looks like?

Cellphone
Is here,
Waiting
for you…
Please,
Call me at
Anytime!

Eyes
Touch
Smells
Skin
Rush
Deep breath...

At the subatomic level,
Love is just a...
Mathematical formula
Of attraction,
Doesn't matter...

Love has no time
Speed
Logic
Reason
Explanation
Rules
Doesn't make sense

IT IS INSIDE
BLIND
SITE
MIND
TIMELESS
HELP ME!!!

32

Your kisses make me blue,
Your kisses make me blue,
I could
Never
Never
Never
Ever
Forget…

ME + YOU = LOVE

34

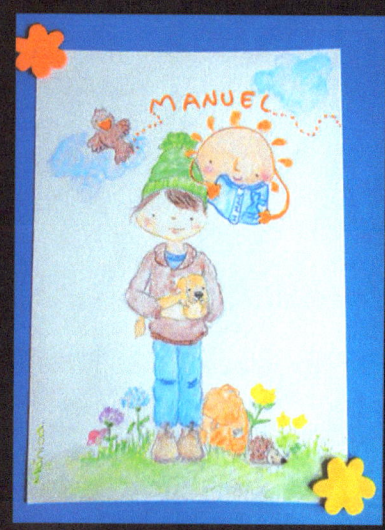

**When in you are in Love,
Our senses get stronger,
Our reasons weak...**

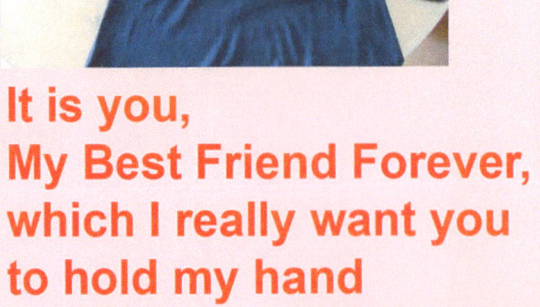

It is you,
My Best Friend Forever,
which I really want you
to hold my hand
at the end…

monica-ilustraciones.blogspot.com

http://www.amapolita.es/?p=2298#.VqjVnvpLBAQ.whatsapp

Mónica Ortiz García, nació en Badajoz,
España y frontera con Portugal.
Estudió en la Escuela de Artes y Oficios de Badajoz.
Desde pequeña creció rodeada
de papeles, lápices y cuentos.
Ha realizado ilustraciones para la enseñanza infantil,
tienda on-line de juguetes, tarjetas para librerías,
láminas y bolsas personalizadas.
Actualmente trabaja como ilustradora freelance.
Desde 2008 hasta la actualidad
expone y comparte sus trabajos en su BLOG

Colaboró ilustrando la portada del libro
Puzzle del poeta Adonis Brunet publicado
en Francia.Asi como colaboraciones
en exposiciones colectivas ,Libroteca El gato de
Cheshire (Zaragoza-España) y Todos por Nepal".

She lives in Badajoz, Spain

Mónica Ortiz García"
e-mail; ortizgarciamonica@gmail.com

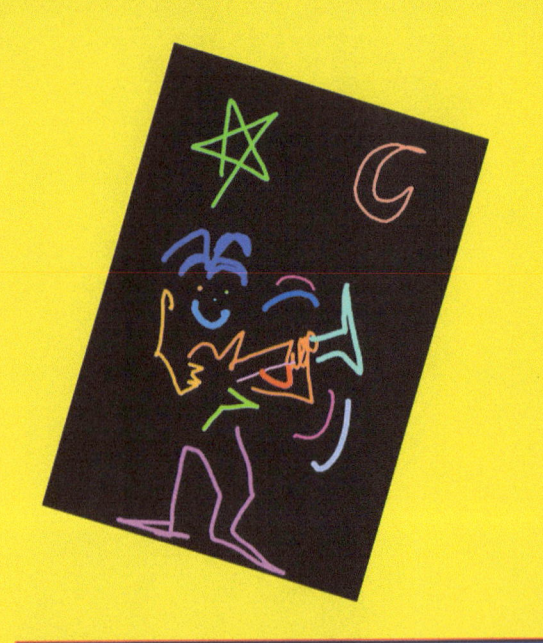

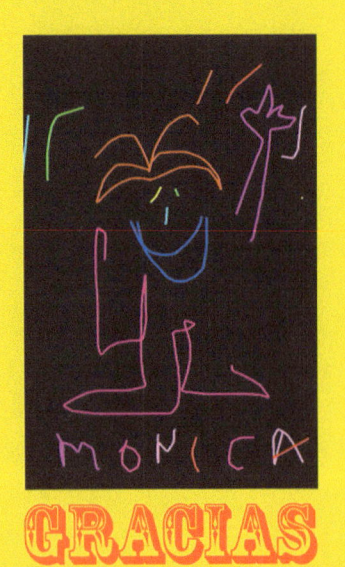

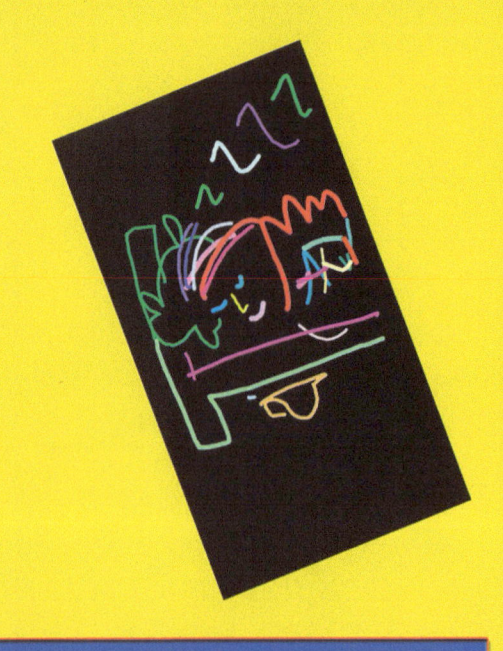

GRACIAS

Wagner Anarca Books Collection Released USA

- Drawings Sketchbook 2009 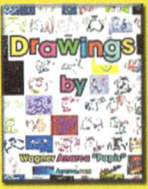
- Drawings 2010 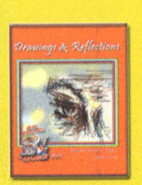
- Drawings & Reflections 2011 
- Anarca, My Rock Band... 2012 
- Just Drawings 2013 
- Lear2Draw 2013 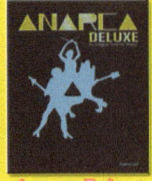
- Anarca, DeLuxe 2013 
- Wagner Anarca 2014 
- Sky Ching 2014 
- Stokes of Genius 6 Contributor pg 70 Just Walkin pg 6 Introduction 2015 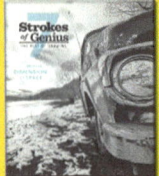
- Stokes of Genius 7 Contributor pg 72 Mister Zzzz 2015 
- Love 2016

Wagner Anarca Discography Released Brazil & USA

- Vinyl Double LP Anarca Live in Brazil 1980/86 Brazil
- Vinyl EP Anarca "Ruidos e Superstição" Brazil 
- Vinyl LP São Power produced by Celso Barbieri Brazil 
- CD Anarca "The Best of the Past" Live 80/96 USA 
- CD Anarca "A Tribute to Vinnie Moore and Rush" Live 93 USA 
- CD Solo Wagner Anarca "Stephaniee's Song" USA 
- CD God's Gift "Larger Than Life" 1997 USA 
- CD "God's Gift II" 1999 USA 
- CD "Keyboard Music I" Wagner Anarca 2000 USA 
- Cd "Keyboard Music II" 2001 Wagner Anarca USA 

INFO@ANARCA.COM

CPSIA information can be obtained
at www.ICGtesting.com
Printed in the USA
LVHW070014040622
720442LV00002B/33